S.I.D.

CHANGING THE LANGUAGE AND VALUE OF CONFLICT FOR BUSINESS LEADERS

Written by **Norman Kerfoot**

Illustration by **Andrew Morris**

I would like to acknowledge the advice and support of numerous clients, colleagues and friends: Ian Henderson, Kisane Prutton, Paul Kettlewell, Andrew Morris, Chris and John Kerfoot for creating 'The S.I.D. Theme Tune' and of course my wife Sue, for her adoption of SID and for generally putting up with me.

INTRODUCTION

Disputes, differences and conflicts are a natural result of your daily interaction with the members of your organisation and with people from other companies with whom you do business.

Despite the fact that they occur regularly; differences are often perceived as something that should be avoided. If handled correctly they can help to trigger stronger working relationships, improve productivity and create an environment that promotes the development of innovative solutions.

S.I.D. is a simple but highly effective model that will enable you and your people to gain the maximum value from divulging and exploring differences.

S.I.D. allows differences to be expressed and explored in a less confrontational way.

It enables managers and leaders to change the language available to them to effectively deal with conflicts.

In getting to know and understand S.I.D. you will be able to apply the methodology in a way which works best for you.

"Norman introduced me to SID over 10 years ago! The concept of SID is simple, yet as I have developed several teams over the years and introduced SID to them, the effect has been dramatic. SID engenders a safe and common environment for the team, becomes part of our language "I have a SID". This has helped to produce open, challenging and progressive businesses."

Richard Adams

International Development Director, Balfour Beatty plc

USING THIS BOOK

By the time you have finished this book you will be able to:

- Recognise the power of difference.
- Know how to apply a trusted model and approach.
- Ensure that in the future you, your people and your business will profit from exploiting differences.
- Understand that staying silent in conflict situations reduces opportunities for personal and business growth.

This publication is not intended to be an academic thesis (although there is a little bit of theory thrown in) It is designed to be a short, fun and practical guide for anyone who is employed in a leadership position in business.

This book takes approximately 20 minutes to read. We recommend that you read it through once and then use it for reference.

We hope that you enjoy the experience and that S.I.D. becomes a valuable tool and friend.

Welcome to the World of

S.I.D.

CONTENTS

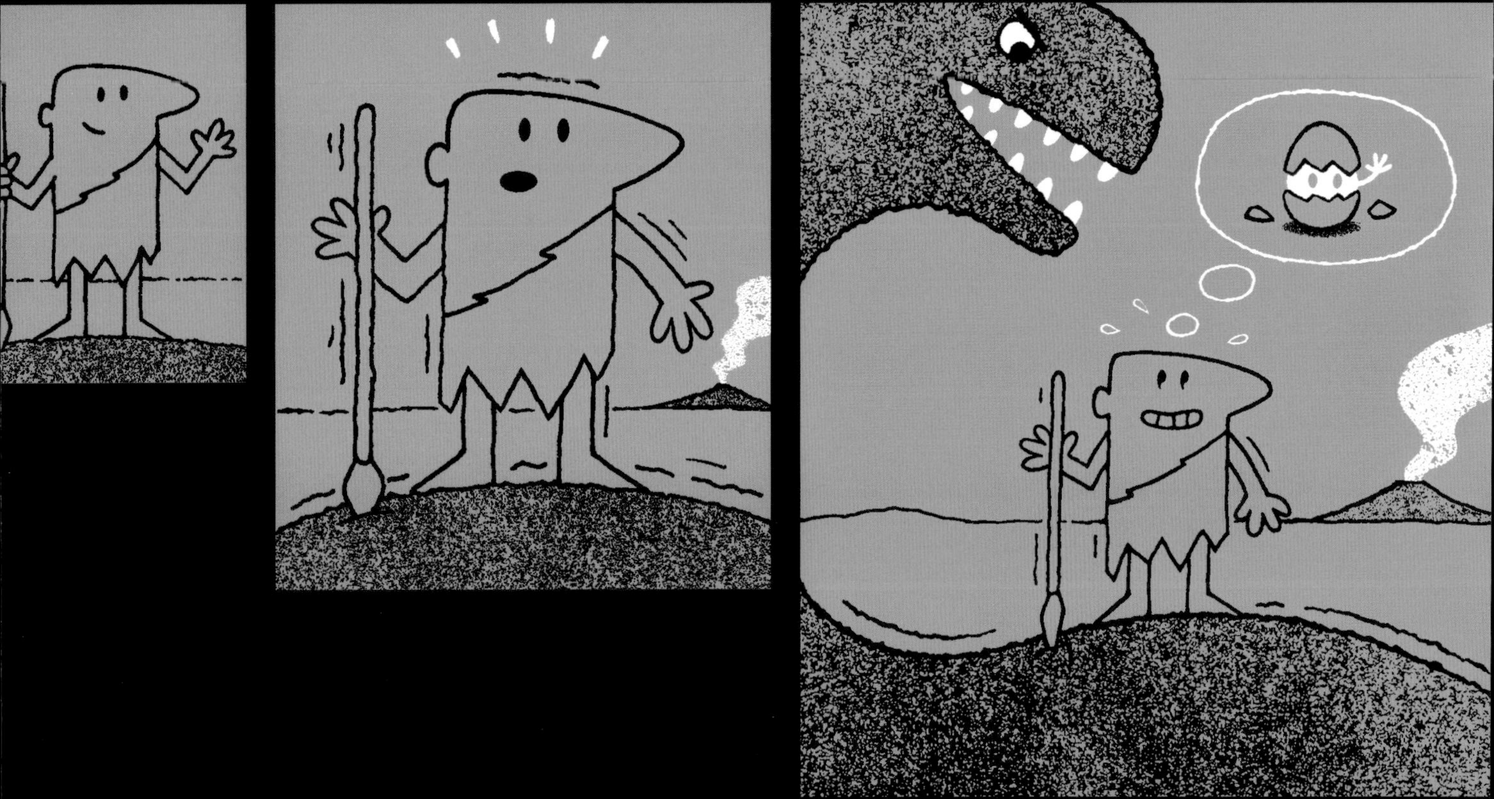

INTRODUCING S.I.D.

S.I.D. is an acronym which stands for:

- **SILENT**
- **INTERNAL**
- **DISCUSSIONS**

You may not instantly recognise him, but we all have one. He has been a part of your life for as long as you can remember. He can pop up at any time and in any situation; it might be during a meeting, dealing with your partners, or talking with colleagues. Still not sure who he is? Well, SID is responsible for those important discussions you have in your head but don't give voice to.

You may be thinking at this point 'so what?' But the discussions that you have with SID are actually very important. If used properly SID can be particularly beneficial, especially when openly introduced to the other people with whom you work. He can also be potentially unhelpful and disruptive if he is ignored or used inappropriately.

SID is likely to be more active or on his guard when your anxiety levels are raised, so expect him to turn up in situations like internal meetings, workshops, interviews and performance reviews. He is also likely to be present when you are working with people for the first time; such as dealing with joint venture members or partners.

In these circumstances, when you feel anxious or guarded about a situation, you may be tempted to silence or ignore your SID in order to avoid the issue. By taking the easy route and staying silent, you risk setting a pattern for future interactions that will follow a similarly unfulfilling process.

For instance; a group of your managers are having a meeting. On the agenda is the relocation of some or all of the staff. Few in the meeting believe it to be good idea. Nobody questions the proposal so the move is approved and goes ahead. The net result being that a poor decision is made with serious implications in terms of working efficiency, costs, morale and staff turnover.

This situation was allowed to develop because group members were having the kinds of discussions in their heads that they *should* have been having openly across the table. These are **Silent Internal Discussions (S.I.D.'s)**

SID allows differences and conflicts to be expressed in a less confrontational way. It helps managers and leaders to change the language available to them to deal with conflicts. In this situation, if SID had been introduced as an active part of the manager's vocabulary, a richer debate would have resulted with a better quality decision.

HOW SID APPEARS:

NORMAL RELAXED STATE

INSTINCT TRIGGERED BY EXPOSURE TO SITUATION

INSTINCT EVOLVES INTO FULLY FORMED SID

SILENT INTERNAL DISCUSSIONS BEGIN

A WORD FROM SID

Now that you have found out a little bit more about who I am, why I appear and how I operate, am I starting to sound a little more familiar?

I'm sure you will admit that from time to time when you are feeling anxious about a particular situation, I am sometimes silenced or ignored. Deep down you know that I never completely shut up or go away. I just become more anxious and active, bubbling under the surface and waiting to pop up when you least expect it.

I just want to help whenever I can. I think of myself as being a bit like a spanner. I can be very useful helping things to come together and apart in an orderly and disciplined way.

But if I am not allowed to help, I can behave more like a spanner in the works – **jamming any progress!**

Lets take a look at some examples of me in action:

SILENT AND DEADLY

IMMATURE SIDs IN AN EXECUTIVE TEAM

A business is expanding and many of the senior managers are promoted to the Board. Some of the behaviours and styles of the new Board members are the same as they were when they were operating in Senior Management.

THE DIRECTOR's SID:

THE M.D.'s SID:

A CONFLUENCE OF SIDs – A BUSINESS WITH A LOW WIN RATE

A previously successful business has lost its last 5 major bids spanning in excess of 12 months. The Executive Team discuss openly and record that they need to review their bid winning approach.

The team's discussion continues with occasional hints at what their SID's are actually thinking. Eventually the SID's of the Executive Team members coalesce, placing the blame outside of their ranks.

A collective SID can sometimes occur when groups choose to adopt a belief in order to avoid accepting an unpalatable truth, namely that the business offer and possibly the business needs drastic reshaping.

SID AT WORK – A TYPICAL MEETING WITH ROOM FOR IMPROVEMENT

BUSINESS SITUATION

You are involved in a debate in which differences of opinion represent an opportunity or threat.

YOU HAVE A SID ABOUT SOMETHING

Silent Internal Discussions warn you of the real or potential conflicts, opportunities or risks.

BEHAVIOUR

SID drives your behaviour e.g. you either withdraw from the debate and be quiet, or voice your SID in a confrontational way.

RESPONSE

Your colleagues involved in the debate respond, by either retaliating to or mirroring your behaviour.

OUTCOME

The result is a partially considered decision, a damaged relationship and an unhelpful formula established for the next meeting.

THE NEXT MEETING?

Assuming there will *be* another one. The pattern of behaviour has been established, so expect to experience more of the same.

SID AT WORK – THE SAME MEETING WITH THE SID APPROACH INCLUDED

BUSINESS SITUATION

Introducing the concept of using SID gives you licence to announce and for others to recognise and understand your resulting behavior.

YOU HAVE A SID ABOUT SOMETHING

In seeking to avoid destructive conflict by staying silent, we lose the opportunity to profit from open and constructive dialogue.

BEHAVIOUR

As leaders, you need to set the tempo by working towards openly disclosing your predominant SID in the correct way.

RESPONSE

If we stay silent on conflict we are more likely to stay silent during the next one. This can result in increasing personal and business opportunity cost.

OUTCOME

Disclosing and discussing your SID, demonstrates acceptable behaviour while preventing sub-optimisation and damage to the relationship.

THE NEXT MEETING?

Before you next meet, check that the formula that you have adopted has worked for both parties which will strengthen the relationship for the future.

The Conflict Volcano represents the continuum of differences; from indifference through to open destructive conflict.

If we believe that:

- **Conflict occurs naturally.**
- **Unless dealt with effectively it will not go away but will simply escalate.**
- **It must be dealt with at an appropriate and early point in time and place, using a trusted model such as SID.**

SID allows you to use an accepted model to derive the benefits and avoid the disadvantages of conflict.

If minor differences are allowed to escalate to the open conflict stage, a cooling off period, followed up by SID sessions may be required. However, this is unlikely to fully restore the relationship. SID should preferably be used for prevention rather than cure.

SID AND THE THEORY OF CONFLICT

Follett (1995) one of the thinkers in the field of conflict management and negotiation, wrote:
"Think of (conflict) not as warfare but the appearance of difference, difference of opinion, of interests. For that is what conflict means – difference".

In the area of human behaviour with regard to conflict, there seem to be four fundamental principles:

1. Conflict occurs naturally
Coser (1956) wrote:
"No group can be entirely harmonious. Groups require disharmony as well as harmony, dissociation as well as association; and conflicts within them are by no means altogether disruptive factors... Far from being necessarily dysfunctional, a certain degree of conflict is an essential element".

2. Conflict does not naturally disappear if not tackled. It may submerge if only to re-emerge more strongly in a new situation between the parties.

Follett (1998) recognised the destructive consequences of silencing conflict, noting that:
"The ignoring of differences is the most fatal mistake in politics or industry or international life: every difference that is swept up into a bigger conception feeds and enriches society; every difference which is ignored feeds on society and eventually corrupts it".

3. The behaviour you decide to use will generate a reciprocal behaviour from others.
The behaviour we benefit or suffer from will generate a response from us in kind which can be overt or hidden. Overbearing managers receive little obvious resistance, although meetings are compliant, things don't get done. An overbearing Director will find that his turnover of independent and resourceful senior managers is higher than elsewhere in the business. This is a more obvious measure of the withdrawal of labour than the first example. It is not who they are but how you treat them, that will dictate how your people respond and the profit and deficit you get.

4. The need for a safe space.

The brain has only a finite amount of processing power, the use of which it protects. If we believe that conflict is harmful its capacity will be engaged in self preservation and not in finding creative solutions.

Neuroscience developments reinforce the fact that our basic instinct is to fight or flee. Our self preservation antennae are sensitised to detect the slightest threat. SID situations are risky and we are drawn to situations which are more likely to make us look good. In order to avoid the fight or flee reflex and benefit from disclosing differences, participants must feel safe. This is the role of leadership.

Neuroscience advises that social pain is as real to us as physical pain. If SID's are disclosed in a relaxed environment we can enjoy the experience. Not only do we avoid the flight flee response, our brain also has more processing power and is more disposed to using it in creating innovative solutions rather than focusing on our own safety.

If we believe that a conflict or potential conflict represents an opportunity, the environment for this to take place needs to be safe for the parties involved, there must not be any personal repercussions for disclosing a SID and that any disclosure will be valued.

The next section gives more detail on the leadership role. The benefits for those who have been afforded licence to behave in this way have been documented by people such as Daniel Goleman the author of emotional intelligence. Without exaggerating the potential benefits of using SID; it increases the association of your people with your organisation. Gallup's Employee Engagement work shows 3.9 times per share growth rate compared with organisations in the same sector with lower engagement.

If this background research interests you, please check the references section at the back of this book.

Strong relationships are based on honesty and clear knowledge of our strengths, weaknesses and beliefs. Those who avoid conflict restrict their personal growth.

Businesses who avoid conflict, falsely conform, preventing their people from expressing dissenting opinions. This reduces creativity and competitiveness which will diminish the business and its people. This situation is particularly true in groups under pressure; such as underperforming projects and joint ventures who seek comfort in passive conformity.

If we accept these four principles as a reasonable basis for dealing with conflict, we can start to focus on the opportunity it offers rather than the risk.

Not only is conflict essential to societies and groups, social scientists studying productive personal relationships have found it to be a core component of mature organisations. Walton (1969) explains that the benefits of conflict include increased motivation and energy to accomplish tasks, greater innovativeness, a better understanding of one's own position and heightened awareness of one's own identity.

THE FOUNDATION

Senge (1990) promotes the practice of balancing advocacy and inquiry to facilitate learning in organisations. Advocacy involves stating one's views (expressing SID) inquiry involves asking questions to understand another's views (discovering their SID).

When people practice advocacy and inquiry together, they shift the goal from individual to joint problem solving and then making decisions. This means we move from trying to win an argument to working with others to find the best solution. Senge argues that most managers are trained to be advocates.

For them to incorporate inquiry into how they interact, they need not only to inquire into what is behind another person's views but also to learn to state their own views in a way that invites others to ask questions about them. In order to use SID effectively you will need certain beliefs and competencies.

The beliefs and competences of a leader in this situation over and above consummate business skills are:

BELIEF THAT

- Conflict enables improvement.
- Respect for others and yourself is a right.
- It is acceptable to have alternative answers to the same questions.
- Honesty pays, always.

COMPETENCE

- To listen generously (switch off your own SID and listen respectfully to the SIDs of others first).
- To understand and appreciate differences, you need to practice true enquiry.
- To remain calm when coping with complexity.
- To be candid and clear in communicating and that the self esteem of all concerned has been maintained.

For a conflict to have been successfully managed, the parties:

- Will believe that their relationship has benefited from the experience.
- That the issue is in the process of being resolved.
- That they are better able to handle the next challenge they will face and ideally look forward to the next occasion. There will certainly be one.

CONFLICT MANAGEMENT STRATEGIES

**We all have different approaches to dealing with conflict.
We have observed that there are six generic strategies:**

1. Silencing

Silencing SID... Not saying anything leaves both parties in the dark or uncertain about where the relationship stands.

2. Suppressing or Glossing over

A half-hearted disclosure of SID, not dealing with the real issues. Once glossed over a difference is difficult to reintroduce.

3. Dismissing

When dismissing or ignoring either your own or someone else's SID, you risk the strong likelihood that the situation will deteriorate.

4. Patching up

A partial solution to a problem will eventually lead a partial SID to escalate – albeit more slowly than if completely ignored.

5. Confronting

Aggressively highlighting a difference can make another person's SID dive for cover. This often results in an escalation later in the conflict.

All of these approaches make it difficult for any further discussions, resolution and benefit to flow.

6. Disclosing

Disclosing SID and using the license afforded by using him, gives you the best chance of:

- **Avoiding escalation.**
- **Deriving the value from the difference.**
- **Strengthening relationships for the next time.**
- **Demonstrating to others how it is done.**
- **Looking forward to future differences between you.**

The way that you deal with conflict is a positive demonstration of leadership. You demonstrate this by your behaviour, thereby giving license to your colleagues and team. This will have a significant impact on the maturity of your business.

Disclosing SID demands courage!

USING SID – GETTING IT OVER THE NET

You have been introduced to SID and have looked at some typical examples of him in action. You have looked at how SID can quickly escalate into conflict if the advice that he gives us is either suppressed or ignored. You also understand that in adopting a more candid approach by disclosing your SID, you can maximise the benefits from discussing your differences. This approach also helps to significantly eradicate negative patterns of communication in the workplace.

This is all very well I hear you say, understanding who and what SID is, how and why he appears and realising the potential benefits of using him is one thing. The big question remains; just how do you actually begin to introduce and implement SID?

Anyone for Tennis?

Using SID is very much like playing a game of tennis. You need at least two people to play, you need to understand the rules, use the right equipment and play in an appropriate setting. By adopting the correct approach when using SID, the net result (if you pardon the pun) will be a more rewarding and enjoyable experience, with the increased likelihood of participants looking forward to the next session.

A Word from the Umpire

So, for instance – when you have read this book and are (hopefully) keen to start using SID to test out the theories that we have discussed, it helps if everybody understands how to play at the outset; so make sure that you take the time to properly introduce your colleagues to the concept of SID. You might get them to read the book (ahem a SID – ideally their own copies) and explain that this is a methodology that you think would be useful for you all to use. So that when you are ready to hit the court and practice with your SID, the rest of your team is ready to do likewise.

Booking the Court

As with making arrangements to play tennis you will need to book an appropriate time and place in order to get the most out of your SID sessions. For instance, it might be a good idea to introduce a SID break into your meetings. It is generally not ideal to do this at the end of a meeting as this will not allow sufficient time to adequately deal with any issues that may be raised. You may as a result be forced to trudge off mid-game due to 'insufficient light'.

First Service

It is also advisable to choose a lower risk situation and subject when using SID for the first time. You might want to start off with a colleague or team of people who are quite well known to you. This will reduce the risk of introducing the concept of SID and would help to ensure that the disclosure would not be too damaging at this early stage. It is very important that you take the initiative by electing to disclose your SID first rather than inviting others to take the first step. In doing so you underline your position of leadership by willingly demonstrating the appropriate level of risk taking. This sets a positive example that will help to galvanise your working relationships.

You could start off by saying something along the lines of: 'A SID I'm having at the moment is about...' then serve it over the net towards your 'playing partner'. Once you have served your SID, the object of the exercise is to explore the issue that you have raised by 'having a rally' and knocking it around for a while.

When you have reached the point where you both feel that the subject has been covered adequately, it will be time for 'new balls' and your playing partner will take a turn by serving their SID (if they have one). You will respond similarly by listening carefully to and discussing the SID that they have raised.

Order of Play

Another important point is to ensure that your playing partners understand the *type* of game you are about to play. You may notice that in using the tennis analogy, emphasis has been placed on the word 'game' rather than 'match'. If you approach your SID sessions with an aggressive, match-winning mentality, the temptation will be to try and 'serve an ace' in a bid to secure a cheap point. In doing so, you will miss out on the opportunity for all parties involved to benefit from disclosing their differences through the use of SID and improve their 'level of play'. The object isn't to try to win the argument. It is to optimise the chances of reaching a successful solution for all concerned.

If you take a match winning approach to sessions the result will be that your playing partner/s either stay silent on the subject (take their ball home) or mirror your behaviour by hitting an equally aggressive return. This pattern of behaviour is likely to result in a generally brief and unrewarding experience.

Poor Service

While it is bad practice to adopt an aggressive approach when using SID, you must also avoid the trap of over compensating and being too tentative. If your serve is too weak your SID may be misinterpreted in some way, disregarded, or may not even make it over the net. Remember! Your SID should never be half heartedly disclosed.

Using SID is all a question of approach; try to think of it more like this...

...than this

Practice Court

Naturally the process of using SID will feel a little awkward at first, and of course there will always be the odd ding-dong rally or disputed line call along the way, but once you begin to disclose your SID, you will notice that the more you use it the easier it becomes.

So as you and your team become more comfortable with practice, not only will your general SID skill and fitness levels improve, but regular use will also help to positively shape the operational and cultural fitness of your organisation.

THE ACTIVITY LEVEL OF SID – TAKING THE PLUNGE

As already mentioned SID is more in evidence when your level of anxiety is at its highest, i.e. working with new people, new teams, projects etc. The illustration (right) uses diving as an analogy to show that – when 'taking the plunge' with SID you are faced with a similar type of risk/reward scenario.

Expressing your SID when dealing with conflict is very much like performing a dive, the greater degree of difficulty (or tariff) you choose to execute, the greater the level of risk and reward. The key factor that determines success or failure (in both disciplines) is the level of maturity (or diving skill) of the individual and team.

As you can see, the less experienced you are at dealing with conflict, the larger the zone of risk, the more accustomed you are to dealing with conflict and differences, (or indeed, performing a Forward 2½ Somersault with Twist and Pike) the higher your level of maturity (diving skill). So that even in higher risk situations, you will be more likely to perform, creating less of a splash within the optimum area of performance which we like to call:

'The Zone of Reward'

In terms of conflict management individuals with lower levels of maturity and experience may be tempted to take a risk when expressing their SID. They may as a result dive from the highest board in the hope of securing a greater level of reward; but without the necessary levels of experience or practice behind them the 'Zone of Risk' is at its largest, so that the chances of their SID developing into a damaging conflict (or 'belly flopping') are commensurately higher.

Conversely, an experienced person may decide to dive in with an issue that is comfortably within their conflict solving capabilities, by playing it safe in a bid to reduce their 'Zone of Risk' but in doing so they simultaneously diminish their 'Zone of Reward'.

THE RISK / REWARD BALANCE

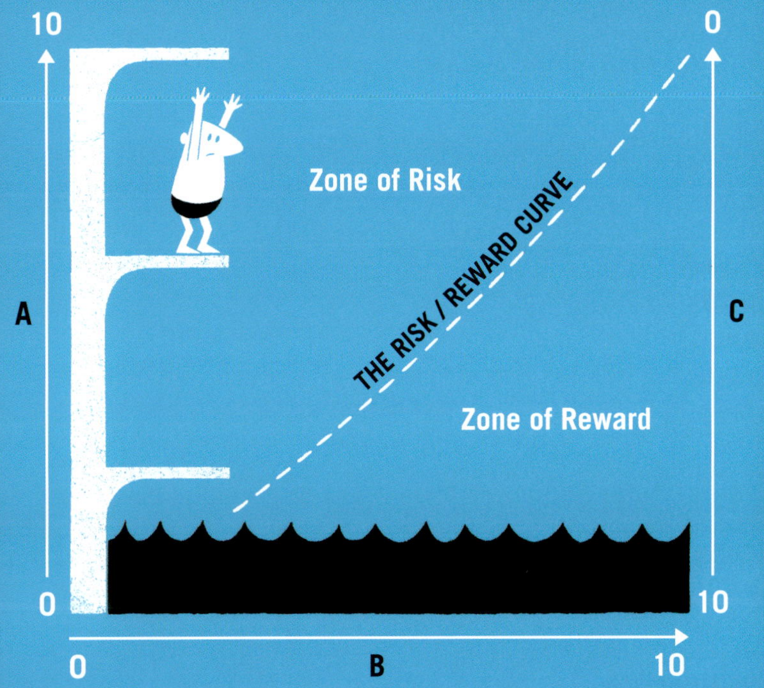

A: level of anxiety, threat or investment in a situation (tariff)
B: level of maturity (diving skill) **C:** Activity level of SID

LEADERSHIP AND CLIMATE CONTROL

As the leader in your organisation, you know that it is part of your responsibility to optimise not only your own performance, but also the performance of your people. One of the ways to achieve this is to demonstrate the appropriate level of risk taking. This can be helped by using SID.

The response you can expect when introducing SID to colleagues, will depend strongly on the cultural atmosphere or climate of the organisation in which you work.

Here are some of the organisational responses you may encounter when introducing SID:

Organisations characterised by a command and control style have many unmentioned and unresolved conflicts. Those that have expressed SID have generally been sanctioned. As a result they go quietly about their business. Examples are strongly hierarchical organisations such as some of the large management consultancies.

Some organisations refuse to accept that any such differences exist within their boundaries. External challenges are seen as wrong. Examples are some Far Eastern companies and organisations established by strong entrepreneurs.

Some organisations who know there are differences, sometimes express them but little changes. As a result, people feel frustrated, poorly utilised and remain trapped in their setting. Examples are some public sector organisations.

We believe that part of your role as a business leader, is to work towards creating the kind of organisational climate where SID can thrive.

AN APPROACH AND EXERCISE

Try this exercise with your team to familiarise them with SID. Keep a record and chart your progress by answering the questions at the end of this session.

Introduce the idea of SID to your colleagues and partners in a safe, low risk meeting where you are able to lead the learning. Manage their expectations, in that, as with any new skill it may feel obvious, uncomfortable and messy at first.

Try limiting the use of SID to a specific subject on the agenda, such as the accuracy of sales forecasts, management information or to review a decision made during a previous meeting. At the time, how did we deal with the unknown SIDs around the subject? How could the process and outcome have changed if we had used SID during that occasion?

SID will be readily adopted by people if the correct environment and leadership is in place. This will increase team engagement, the quality of decision making and certainty of outcomes.

Suggested phrases when using SID:

- 'My SID is this'...
- 'How would it be if we exchanged SIDs?'
- 'Let me understand your SID'

Suggested phrases to avoid when using SID:

- 'May I respectfully suggest...'
- 'Without wishing to offend...'
- 'That SID is incorrect, irrelevant, been explored'

Note: *always* stick to the facts of a situation.

Try and persevere with this new method of working for subsequent meetings and it will quickly become a habit. Review its effectiveness and agree any changes to maximise benefits to the team.

Build up a record of SID and the insights he has given both to you and your colleagues. You could also create a personal record of when you have or haven't used SID and record the outcomes. (example overleaf)

Situation	What I thought (my SID)	What I actually said or did	Outcome

Start to use SID in more of your everyday interactions. Remember to choose the right moment, situation and appropriate language to make the disclosure and to demonstrate leadership.

The questions you might use with your team to review their use of SID may include:

- Where have your SIDs and the SIDs from others made an impact?
- Was there an occasion where SID was not disclosed and there was a negative outcome?
- Why did you disclose or not disclose your SID?
- Where you did disclose your SID, how did you do it and what was the result?

AND FINALLY

Here are a few points to bear in mind:

It is important to be mindful that SID exists. Be aware of situations that can trigger him.

When speaking with someone, you are speaking to their SID, based on their own point of view.

An undisclosed SID is an impediment to learning and of new ways of doing things. This inhibits us from being open to new experiences and better performance.

Awareness of your own SIDs gives you more room to manoeuvre and helps you to make innovative choices. SID needs to know that you will disclose his thoughts and sayings in your interactions with your colleagues. This has the following effects:

- It disarms SID. This makes him less dangerous both to you and to your colleagues.
- It gives license to you and to your colleagues to disclose and to disarm their SID.

- It turns SID into a force for good and open communication.
- Allows you to maximise the zone of opportunity.

When SIDs collide, see it as an opportunity for an early resolution of a hidden conflict which would, in any case have emerged at a later date. Always remember that conflict never goes away.

Disclosing SID in a supportive atmosphere galvanises the group and creates a safe zone for participants.

SID provides you as a leader with a vocabulary and model to safely demonstrate how conflict can be turned into a source of opportunity. It also helps you create an ethos which recognises differences, is energised and focussed on deep seated improvement.

Remember as a leader, continue taking risks beyond your comfort zone. It is important to build on any reciprocal SIDs disclosed by others.

LINKS AND FURTHER SUPPORT

We hope that you have enjoyed this book and that you will soon be using SID profitably.

To become a member of the SID community, simply log onto the website at www.thelandofsid.com Registration is quick, easy (and free).

Once you have registered we will send you infrequent updates on SID's progress, including the very latest information. Your SID might be telling you at this point that this is a sales ploy (and he would be right) but it is primarily to help you maximise your use of SID and to exchange information and experiences for the benefit of other members of the SID community.

Every quarter there will be a prize to the member who submits the most valuable approach, tip or SID related snippet, simply visit **'The Trading Post'** section of our website for more details on how to get involved.

Once again, welcome to the World of SID!

Coser, L.A. (1956)
'The functions of society conflict.' Glencoe, Free Press, 11, p.31.

Follett, M.P. (1995)
'Creative collaboration' in Pauline Graham, ed, Prophet in management. Boston, Harvard Business School Press, p.67.

Follett, M.P. (1998)
The new state. University Park, Pennsylvania State University Press, p.40.

Senge, P. (1990)
The fifth discipline: The art and practice of learning organization. New York, Doubleday, p.198-202.

Baumaster Roy F; Bratslavsky, Ellen; Finkenaur, Catrin; Vohs, Kathleen D. (2001)
'Review of General Psychology' Vol 5 (4) Dec 2001, 323-370.

Frederickson Barbara L. (2001)
'The role of positive emotions in positive psychology: The broaden--and-build theory of positive emotions' American psychologist, Vol 56 (3), Mar, 218-226.

David Rock; Jeffrey Schwartz. (2006)
'The Neuroscience of leadership, Breakthroughs in brain research explain how to make organizational transformation succeed' Strategy + Business Issue 43 2006.

Dr. Matthew Lieberman and Dr. Naomi Eisenberger. (2008)
University of California, Los Angeles 'The pains and pleasures of social life: a social cognitive neuroscience approach' Neuro leadership Journal 2008.

Tania Singer; Ben Seymour; John P O'Docherty; Klaas E Stephan; Raymond J. Dolan & Chris D. Frith (2006)
'Empathic neural responses are modulated by the preceived fairness of others' Nature 439, 26 January 2006. 466-469.

Carter Elizabeth J; Pelphrey Kevin A. (2008)
Carnegie Mellon University, Pittsburgh, PA USA. 'Friend or foe brain systems involved in the perception of dynamic signals of menacing and friendly social approaches'. Social Neuroscience, 3:2 151-163. Psychology Press 24 May 2008.

Gallup website (2011)
'Employee engagement, a leading indicator of Employee engagement' 21st April 2011.

Senge, P. (1990)
'The fifth discipline: The art and practice of learning organization' New York, Doubleday, p.198-202.

Walton, R.E. (1969)
'Interpersonal peacemaking: confrontations and third party consultation.' Mass Addisons-Wesley, p.5.